# My Prairie Year

*Based on the Diary of Elenore Plaisted*

# My Prairie Year

*Based on the Diary of Elenore Plaisted*

by **Brett Harvey**

illustrated by **Deborah Kogan Ray**

SCHOLASTIC INC.
New York Toronto London Auckland Sydney

for Robert and Katie
B. H.

for Margery
D. K. R.

Text copyright © 1986 by Brett Harvey.
Illustrations copyright © 1986 by Deborah Kogan.
All rights reserved. Published by Scholastic Inc., 730
Broadway, New York, NY 10003, by arrangement with
Holiday House, Inc.
Printed in the U.S.A.
ISBN 0-590-46592-9

7 8 9 10    08              0 1 2/0

When my mother's mother, Elenore Plaisted, was nine years old in 1889, she and her family moved from Lincoln, Maine, to a homestead in Dakota Territory. Years later, aware that she had been part of a unique piece of American history, she wrote down what she could remember in a little brown notebook for her daughter, my mother. One of the great pleasures of my own childhood was having my mother dig the notebook out of her cedar chest and read it aloud to me. I never tired of hearing about the ocean of rippling prairie grass, the tornado, the prairie fire, and all the details of the strange life they lived. Because I feel that other children might be as fascinated as I was by my grandmother's Dakota adventure, I've taken her words and shaped them into a story. Although I've added and rearranged things here and there, a good deal of this book is just as my grandmother set it down. She was a writer as well as an artist, so her account was full of vivid images.

When she grew up, Elenore Plaisted became a successful children's book illustrator. She lived in Philadelphia and died in 1938. I think she would have been surprised and pleased to know that her Dakota experience was being shared by so many children in the form of this book. And I know she would have felt that Deborah Kogan Ray's pictures truly capture that experience.

BRETT HARVEY
*September 15, 1985*

Our house on the prairie was like a little white ship at sea. Not a tree, not a bush to be seen—just endless tall grass that billowed in the wind like the waves of an ocean. Our house was set on a small hill and around it was a pond made by rainwater, with a wooden bridge across it. The house was anchored to the ground with a high bank of earth that came up to the windowsills and was covered with grass. "To keep the house from blowing away in a tornado," Daddy said.

Our family had come to the Dakotas from Maine to be what Daddy called "homesteaders." Daddy came out first by himself to find our land and build our house. Then he sent for Mother and me and my little sister, Marjorie, and my baby brother, Billy. We traveled on a big, black train that belched smoke and steam. After what seemed like weeks, the train finally stopped one rainy night in a place called Andover. As we climbed down to the platform, there was Daddy, a black rubber figure stamping toward us, streaming with water and shouting happily, "Hallo! Em! Hallo, you children!"

We felt very strange that first night in our new home. You could see right through the walls of our room, for they were made of pine boards which hadn't been plastered yet. Daddy nailed horse blankets over the bare boards, and Mother put us to sleep on canvas cots. I fell asleep wondering what life would be like in this new place.

I learned that life on the prairie was different from life back home in Maine in every way.

Monday was washday. Mother learned to make a fire in the big kitchen range with soft, queer-smelling coal. My job was to trudge back and forth over the little wooden bridge, bringing back pail after pail of rainwater from our "moat." Then Daddy would empty the buckets into the huge tin washboiler and hoist it up on the range to heat. After the clothes were washed, we emptied the washboiler and filled it up in the same way for rinsing.

Later, Mother would carry the baskets, heavy with wet clothes, out to the clothesline. Marjorie and I would hand her things and she would hang them up. Then Marjorie and I would chase each other through the sweet-smelling sheets and clothes flapping in the sun, the damp ends brushing against our faces.

Tuesday was ironing and mending day. I stood on a soapbox by the ironing board, with my own little iron. It was heavy, but I was strong for my nine years. I ironed the handkerchiefs and towels, which I had sprinkled with water and rolled tight to keep damp.

In the afternoon, I sewed with Mother. Clothes seemed to wear out fast on the prairie and we were always darning stockings and mending underclothes. Mother showed me how to use a darning egg, but I didn't like staying indoors and envied Marjorie and Billy, who were still too young to sew.

On Wednesday we gardened in the morning before it got too hot. Mother had brought packets of seeds from New England, and we planted rows of peas, beets, tomatoes, beans, corn and melons. Watermelons were especially important in the heat of the summer. The water in our well was tepid and we ate watermelon to quench our thirst. No matter how hot it was, the melon always tasted cool and refreshing. We planted the corn in shallow trenches called drills. Things grew so fast on the prairie that in no time the corn shot up over my head. Then we children would play in the shady alleys between the stalks, decorating each other with soft, shining corn silk.

In the afternoons, Marjorie and I sat on boxes in the shade and did the lessons Mother had given us. Mother had to teach us herself because there was no school close enough for us to go to.

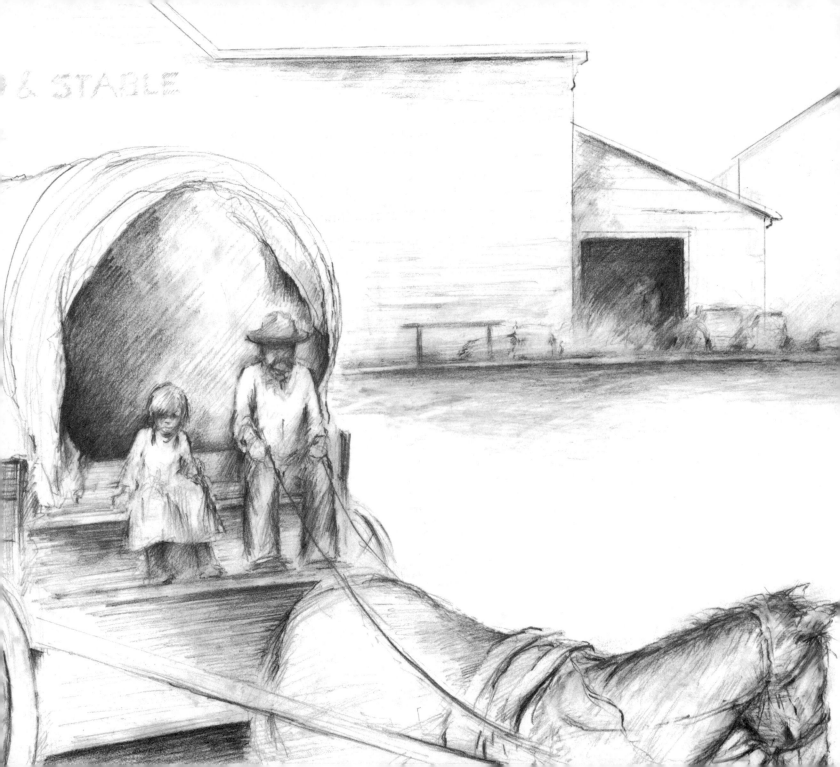

On Thursdays, Daddy and I would ride to Britton to get supplies. We had a funny, horse-drawn wagon with a round canvas top on hooks. Britton was two miles away on a straight road, black as ink. In town, the main street was either very muddy or deep with thick dust. You walked across it on a wobbly boardwalk of planks. The town was no more than a few shacks and a three-story wooden hotel, with six windows in rows of two up the face of it. The hotel proprietor had a daughter, Jennie, who was just my age, and we would sit on the back steps of the hotel and make doll clothes together.

Friday was cleaning day. Father had tried to get a woman from Britton to come and help Mother with the housework, but no one could be found. Women were scarce and needed in their own homes. So we all swept and scrubbed every corner of the house. Even Marjorie and baby Billy had jobs to do.

Saturday was cooking and baking day. All the bread that had been set to rise Friday night was kneaded into enough loaves for the week, and baked. Stacks and stacks of golden brown loaves were set out to cool on a table by the window. Then we wrapped them and packed them in the big wooden bread bin. We baked pans of ginger cookies and pies from dried apples and peaches because there was no fresh fruit on the prairie. In the summer we "put up" the vegetables from the garden. It was hot work, boiling the jars and the vegetables to keep everything clean. But after we were finished, our cellar cupboard was filled with brilliant jars of deep red beets, bright green and yellow beans, golden corn, and delicious, rosy watermelon pickles.

Sundays in the Dakotas were glorious. Sundays meant no work and no lessons except our Sunday School lesson. When that was over, we were free to run wild on the prairie.

On Sundays there was time to ride Dolly, the gentle horse Daddy had bought for Mother. She was chestnut, and her neck curved as if she were always looking at her knees. At first Mother rode her a lot, wearing a dark green riding habit, and sitting gracefully in a sidesaddle. But soon she seemed to have too much work to do to ride Dolly, so we children took to riding her bareback, with nothing but a rope halter. Later, Mother told me I was too old to ride "straddle," but must learn to use the sidesaddle—"like a lady," she said. She made me a long riding skirt out of her own green habit.

In the spring the great ploughing was done and many men came to the farm. The ploughs started out side by side, six or more ploughs in a row, two horses to a plough. The men drove miles in this straight line, getting smaller and smaller in the distance. Then they would turn and come back, and a wide stretch would be finished. The harrows, huge rakes that were drawn over the soil to smooth it, followed in the same way. The prairie grass was short in the spring and violets and other wild flowers grew thick on the black earth. I used to run along ahead of the ploughs, trying to pick as many as I could before they were turned under.

On spring days Mother would let Marjorie and me take a picnic down to the coulee. Coulees are streams, some shallow, some deep, that run through the prairie, unseen until you come right up to them. They make a soft, rustling noise, like something secret hidden in the tall grass.

In the summer the sun was so hot it burnt everything yellow dry. Some days the heat was so intense that we were not allowed outside the shade of the house. One day I saw the horizon swimming in ripples like water and, as I watched, shapes began to appear. I ran to get Daddy.

"Quick, Daddy," I shouted, "an upside-down wagon train is coming!"

Daddy came out of the barn to stand with me, shading his eyes. Across the shimmering horizon, people, horses and wagons were moving—all upside down.

"A mirage," Daddy said.

"What's a mirage and how soon will it get here?" I demanded. He smiled down at me.

"I'm afraid it won't, Elenore, because it's not real. Oh, there's a wagon train all right, but it's much too far away for us to see. What we're seeing is a reflection of it made by rays of sunlight that get bent by the hot air out there."

"Oh," I said, disappointed. That wagon train seemed so real I could almost hear the clip-clop of the horses' hooves and the cries of the children.

At sunset, after one of these scorching days, great clouds began to gather, all reddish brown and orange and flame-colored. They came so close you felt you could touch them, and they were rolling and boiling, but we felt no wind. Suddenly there was a draft of cold air and off in the distance, a snakey black cloud was rushing toward us. The men came running in from the fields shouting "Tornado!" The oxen were turned loose, and we all crowded into the cellar. As we crouched in that dark, quiet place, the sky seemed to tear loose, as if a freight train were passing right over us. When we came out everything was silent and dripping wet, and the house still stood.

In autumn the great thrashing machines came thundering up to the farm for the harvest. The farm was a busy and exciting place, full of men working, shouting and washing themselves boisterously in tin basins out by the well. Women came from miles away to help Mother cook for so many men. Long tables made of boards and sawhorses were set up outside the kitchen, loaded with doughnuts and pies and pots of strong black coffee.

Wheat dust glittered in the air and there were pools of chaff around the thrashing machines. The sheaves of wheat were sucked into the machines and yellow grain came flowing out to be gathered in bags, tied, and stacked on wagons. Then the wagons were driven to the granary and emptied down little square windows high up in the blank face of the granary building. October 18 was my 10th birthday and I spent it driving one of the wagons to and fro between the thrashers and the granary. I felt so important, sitting high on my wagon and cracking my whip over a span of huge farm horses.

One night in the fall I awoke to find Mother shaking me urgently. "Get up, Elenore, quickly, now, and help me with the children." As we woke Marjorie and Billy and wrapped them in blankets, I saw that the room was lit by a red glare from outside the windows. Mother hustled us downstairs and out the door to the cellar. We stood in the doorway for a moment, transfixed by the column of fire towering in the black sky. It was a prairie fire—still far away but being blown toward our place by high winds, and coming closer all the time. Sparks were sailing through the air and dropping onto the barns, the granary, and on the grass around us. We saw the silhouettes of the men against the red sky, beating out the sparks as they fell, and dragging wet blankets up ladders to the barn roof. Mother tucked Marjorie and Billy safely in the cellar and then she whirled away to join the men. I stationed myself outside the cellar door to guard the children and, using a piece of old carpet, beat out any sparks that fell too close.

By now clouds of sparks were falling everywhere. The men were working feverishly and shouting, the horses in the barn were snorting and stamping with fear, and the oxen were being driven in from the coulee where they had been staked out for the night.

Suddenly Mother was beside me, her face grim in the crimson light, her hair and shawl whipping around her. She grabbed me and pulled me against her smokey-smelling body and, as we clung together, we felt a great wave of intense heat and suddenly the wall of fire seemed to be all around us, roaring and crackling. We stood still, too terrified even to scream, waiting to be swallowed up by flames. But the wall of fire swept past us with incredible speed, and then it was gone.

The next morning I looked out on a prairie that was charred black as far as the eye could see. Wisps of smoke curled up here and there where small fires were still smoldering. But standing in the middle of a great yellowish square of ground were our house and barns—scorched, but safe. That square patch of land had been ploughed early in the summer while the grass was still green. It had saved us from being burned.

In the winter the snow was so deep and the cold so terrible that we sat around the enormous cylindrical stove which was red hot, swathed in blankets, overcoats and woolens. We had to put the butter on the stove so that it would melt enough to cut. I cried because of the cold, standing on my soapbox with my arms in the steaming dishwater.

At first the snow looked just the way it had back in Maine. But soon it was coming down so fast and thick we could see only white outside our windows. Daddy said it looked like a blizzard and that it might go on snowing for days. He went out and stretched a strong rope from our front door to the door of the barn. The wind was howling like wolves and the snow kept coming down so heavily that you couldn't see more than a few inches in front of you. Daddy would push the door open with all his might, letting in a great blast of icy, snowy wind, and feel his way blindly along the rope to the barn to feed and water the animals.

The winter days stretched out long and cold and dark and boring. I thought spring would never come.

Then one day a box arrived from Aunt Addie, Mother's sister back in Maine. We unpacked it on the big pine table, exclaiming at all the treasures. There were jars of *real* fruit—apples, oranges and lemons—wools and cottons for new clothes, toys, and, best of all, books and magazines. I was starving for something to read. I drank in the smell of fresh new pages and printer's ink.

There was a special package for Mother with paints and canvases in it. To our surprise, she sat right down and began painting a long spray of pink apple blossoms against a deep blue sky. I knew she was thinking of Maine because there were no apple trees on the prairie. We were all feeling a little homesick, but Mother's apple blossoms made us think spring might come after all.

And spring did come! Overnight, it seemed, the prairie was dotted with pale lavender pasqueflowers. The sky was as blue as the sky in Mother's painting. Tiny dickcissels swayed on top of the weeds and called to each other in high thin chirps. Wild geese flew far overhead, babbling to each other like a crowd of faraway people. Sleepy gophers poked up out of their holes and scanned the sky for hawks.

Even Mother left her washing and came out with us to play in the long grass. We chased her until we were laughing so hard we had to fall down. Then Marjorie said, "Do you think we'll ever go home?"

Mother pulled Marjorie into her lap and looked at me over her head. "We are home," she said.